# LIFE OF ST. OTHMAR

# LIFE OF ST. OTHMAR

## WALAFRID STRABO

Copyright 2025 by Dalcassian Press

All rights reserved. No part of this book may be reproduced in any manner whatsoever without written permission except in the case of brief quotations embodied in critical articles and reviews.

No part of this publication may be reproduced, distributed, or transmitted in any form or by any means, including photocopying, recording, or other electronic or mechanical methods, without the prior written permission of the publisher, except in the case of brief quotations embodied in critical reviews and certain other non-commercial uses permitted by copyright law. For permission requests, write to Dalcassian Press at admin@thescriptoriumproject.com

Translator: Curtin, D.P. (1985-)

ISBN: 979-8-3482-6637-0 (Paperback)
ISBN: 979-8-3482-6636-3 (eBook)
Library of Congress Control Number:

Printed by Ingram Content Group, 1 Ingram Blvd, La Vergne, Tennessee
First Printing 2025, Dalcassian Press, Wilmington, DE

This work is part of a series produced in association with the Scriptorium Project and its community of scholars and translators.
Please visit our website at: www.thescriptoriumproject.com

# Life of St. Othmar (English)

**PROLOGUE.** *To the brothers of the monastery of Saint Gall.*
Having completed the two little books concerning the life and virtues of the blessed Gallus, confessor, according to the faith that has reached us through writing or spoken word, we have composed them with more truth than elegance; at your request, dearest brothers, who are established in the monastery of the same holy Father, and who exhibit a specimen of the fervor he had in divine matters and the sanctity of his purpose, we wish to append the account that has been committed to writing by your assertion and care regarding the studies and virtues of the holy Father Othmar, shown through his merits: which, being full of truth and clear in reasoning, is reiterated by us not for any other reason than because our dearest brother Gozbert, who published this same work, requested that it be done, indeed commanded it, and whom we have gladly sustained in this task, tirelessly and without weariness. Therefore, let this abbreviation of ours suffice for the credulous reader; however, for the incredulous, let him recur to the composition we follow, and if he is grateful, he will not be sluggish in seeking the multiple testimonies of the assembly to faith.

**CHAPTER I.** *How the man of God Othmar was appointed to the sanctity of the life of the cell of Saint Gall and established a regular life there by royal authority.*
Therefore, Othmar, of Alemannic descent, was brought in his youthful age by his brother to Raetia Curiense, and having been established for a long time in the service of Victor, the count of those parts, and exalted in the knowledge of letters, a seeker of virtues and a possessor of praiseworthy morals, he ascended to the degree of priesthood, and having been kindly retained by the aforementioned count,

he was appointed to a certain title of Saint Florinus, confessor. And when the probity of his morals and the purity of holy life were reported far and wide through the sweet rumor of many, a certain Waltramnus, who claimed the desolation of the hermitage where Saint Gall had built his cell as if it had been transmitted to him by hereditary right from his ancestors, requested that the same Othmar be appointed by the aforementioned Victor to oversee that cell; and having been successful in his request, he solemnly entrusted the cell with all that pertained to it to him. And in order that the utility of his desire might better prevail, he set out to King Pippin, presented the same abbot to him, and surrendered the place to the prince by the right of ownership, earnestly requesting that by royal authority Othmar the abbot be appointed to that place anew. To this petition, the aforementioned prince assented, entrusted the place given to him to the venerable man, and commanded that a regular life be established there. And he, having returned, immediately executed the study of good management, constructing suitable dwellings for the monks from all sides, and most diligently reformed the state of that sacred place for the benefit of divine service. He also invited the religious with such liberality to the study of devotion that, from certain donations, he greatly expanded the possessions of the same monastery, and within a few years he decently governed many drawn to the sacred military life by his teaching and care.

**CHAPTER II.** *How he shone with the perfection of holy conversation.*

Having stated these things, let us briefly touch upon the holiness of his life, so that it may clearly be evident to all by what degrees of progress he was elevated to this glory. He was indeed an exceptional follower of frugality, frequently wearing down his body with fasting, so that on the principal days of fasting he would often continue a two-day abstinence as a custom. And against the arrows of temptations, he was fortified with the shields of vigilance, and through the assiduity of prayer he repelled spiritual wickedness. Moreover, he was especially endowed with the grace of supreme humility, so much so that he loved voluntary poverty to such a degree that he fled earthly glory by all means. It was also his custom that if necessity required him to go anywhere for the benefit of the monastery, he would be carried on a humble donkey. Among other things, he had such great concern for the poor that he sought to provide for their care through himself rather than through others. In the work of mercy, which is called almsgiving, he was hardly second to anyone. For the reception of lepers, who were accustomed to remain separated from other men, he established a small hospital not far from the monastery outside the places where the other poor were received, and he devoted himself to their care so diligently that even at night he would often leave the monastery to render service to their infirmity with remarkable devotion. Indeed, washing their heads and feet, he would wipe their festering wounds with his own hands and provide for their necessary sustenance, always recalling in his mind that saying which the just Judge will proclaim to the merciful: "What you did for one of the least of my brothers, you did for me" (Matthew 25). Thus it happened that, with the veneration of all who knew him, he was called the Father of the Poor by many. He was so wholly possessed by the study of mercy that if he saw any poor person suffering from the injury of nakedness, he would often cover the miserable limbs with his own stripped garments, so that sometimes he would return to the monastery without a tunic, clothed only in a cape. For he preferred to reach the garment of eternal incorruption through contempt of present pomp rather than to suffer the shame of future nakedness through the loss of good works.

**CHAPTER III.** *How much mercy he had for the poor.*

At a certain time, coming to King Pippin, he was honorably received, and among other gifts of his generosity, he received seventy pounds of silver to alleviate the needs of his brothers. But as soon as he went out to return to his own, he distributed the greatest part of that money to the poor at the doors of the palace. He scarcely retained a few coins, which he was compelled to keep from the brothers who were with him, with which he later bought a certain territory neighboring the monastery. Not forgetting the Lord's commands, he did not think about tomorrow for his own sake, knowing that a monk should be content with food and clothing: and therefore he chose poverty for himself and his own rather than the superfluous possession of transient things, which burden the mind when freed from them.

**CHAPTER IV.** *How he was affected by many insults from certain wicked men out of zeal for justice, which burned within him.*

Therefore, when the Lord had already decided to repay him with worthy merits, the cunning enemy of all goodness, envious of his good deeds and grieving that others might benefit from his examples, sought to disturb the peace he possessed through much labor in the service of Christ. But although beaten by the winds of temporary adversity, having its root firmly fixed in the rock of truth, the cedar of paradise remained unshaken. For Warinus and Ruadhardus, who at that time governed all of Alamannia, persuaded by the devil and afflicted by the most monstrous disease of greed, violently seized a large part of the possessions of the churches under their control into the domain of their own property. When they had violently reclaimed many possessions of St. Gall, the man of God, Othmar, not longing for earthly possessions, but foreseeing the impending lack of goods for monastic life in that same place, went to King Pippin and exposed to him their tyrannical presumption, equally protesting that he would incur a grave crime if he supported their actions by consenting to them. For this reason, the benevolent prince summoned both of them, threatening that they would completely lose his favor if they did not restore without delay the church of God, which they had unjustly taken away. But they, returning to their homeland, infected by the fault of greed and driven by bestial savagery, disregarded the royal command: they even forced the man of God Othmar, when he wanted to approach the prince again for this matter, to be brought back by force, having secretly sent soldiers after him; and they also persuaded a certain Lambert, who was associated with his brothers by profession, not by the holiness of life, to falsely accuse him of a crime of lust, working to find an occasion to depose him, infamously suspecting his sanctity with such accusations. For this reason, many, unaware of such a treacherous faction, were summoned to the council.

**CHAPTER V.** *How he maintained modesty in the face of the fictitious accusation, and how his accuser was punished.*

Thus, the venerable man, of chaste and unblemished life and mature morals, was placed in the midst of the council, and Lambert, the minister of falsehood, was presented before all in his accusation: having received permission to speak, forgetting the truth, the proponent of falsehood said that he knew a certain woman who had been subjected to the violence of pollution by the blessed man. To this, it is said he gave no response. When he was compelled to respond to many objections, he tempered his speech with such words: "I confess," he said, "that I have sinned excessively in many things, but concerning this accusation of crime, I invoke God, the inspector of my secret." And when they pressed him attentively to clear himself of this deed, secure in mind and free in conscience, he remained silent. And because he knew that the license to accuse was open before the judges, he preferred to please the divine judgment for the sincerity of his heart rather than the human judgment for the excuse of the crime. As soon as it became clear to all that his chastity had been falsely slandered, divine vengeance seized Lambert. For, afflicted by the torment of fevers, he began to gradually lose the strength of his limbs. Thus, with all his limbs losing their uprightness and form, his head bowed to the ground like that of a quadruped, he not only confessed with a terrible deformity of his figure but also with a living voice that he had sinned against the holy man at all times.

**CHAPTER VI.** *How he ended his life under strict custody.*

However, with the wicked counsel begun and more wickedly concluded, the man of God Othmar was enclosed at the villa of Potamus. Since no one was permitted to enter or speak with him, he spent several days without bodily sustenance. And when he was suffering from the prolonged torment of hunger, a certain brother named Peragosus would come at night and provide him with food. Later, however, a certain powerful man named Gozbert, having obtained from the wicked princes that the man of God be entrusted to him, assigned him to custody on a certain island of the Rhine River called Stein, near his estate: where the same holy Father, solely engaged in spiritual exercises, that is, in prayers and fasts, served the Lord more freely because he was freed from human company and worldly cares. By insisting on such and similar works of notable devotion, after not much time had passed, he departed from the troubles of this world to the heavenly breadth of joy, on the sixteenth day before the month of December, and his body remained buried in that same island without corruption for many days thereafter.

**CHAPTER VII.** *How after a long time his body was found incorrupt.*

However, after his passing, ten years later, his brothers were warned by the Lord through a vision to bring the body of their dear Father back to the monastery. Once this was revealed as the counsel of divine will, eleven of those same brothers went at night to the place where the relics of the holy man were kept, and opening the tomb, they found his body untouched by decay, except for the extreme part of one foot, which the water had washed, appearing somewhat discolored as if it were rotten. And with a sufficiently fitting miracle, the first signs of his health became clear, in that both his body was found untouched by corruption and he himself had been freed from sin, which had seemed to overpower him for a time. Therefore, the devoted brothers, more perfectly instructed by this novelty of events, honorably took up the body and, lighting candles, placed one at the head and the other at the feet.

**CHAPTER VIII.** *How wonderfully the storm was calmed during the translation of his body.*

And when they had committed themselves to uncertain depths on the deserted shore, and were earnestly rowing with all speed to return, suddenly such a force of rain and winds broke forth that they scarcely believed they would have an escape. But by the wondrous dispensation of Almighty God and (as we believe) by the merits of the holy man, it happened that even the elements, which seem insensible to us, serving the command of their Creator, felt how great the relics of the man were being carried there. For the sea, stirred by the rainstorm from every side, lifting the waves high, brought no trouble at all to those rowing, but whichever way the ship turned, it lowered the swelling waves by casting off the winds. And so, from every side, pushed back by the weight of the waves, the pouring rain, and the blasts of the winds, as if it were surrounded by a certain skiff, not even a single drop of rain, which heavily inundated from here and there, descended upon it. Moreover, the candles that had been placed at the head and feet of the blessed Father, burning brightly, did not lose the light of their first ignition until his body was carried to the monastery.

**CHAPTER IX.** *About the abundance of drink supplied from heaven, and where his body was buried after the translation.*

Another miracle remains that the Lord revealed to the devoted brothers during the same translation of the sacred body. For when, weary from excessive rowing, they sat down at the hour of refreshment to regain their strength with bodily food, after praising the Lord, and finally were reminded to mix the comforts of drink in a happy feast, one of the servants brought word that no drink was left there, except what was being kept in a small flask, from which scarcely anything could be provided for tasting rather than drinking. They, however, making mention of the Lord's miracles, how He fed a numerous multitude with a few loaves, caused from that same small amount they had to be distributed with love to all who were present. And miraculously, the liquid in that same vessel began to increase so much that with continuous pouring it seemed not to diminish, until those drinking were overwhelmed by the abundance of cups. Therefore, astonished by the novelty of the matter, they rendered due thanks to the Lord, the giver of all good, who had provided them so wonderfully with sufficiency. And as soon as they resumed their journey, the drink ceased in the vessel. And when they had reached the desired port of the shore, the brothers who had come to meet them with praises of God recounted what had happened in order; and having celebrated a common joy, they honorably transported the body of the holy man to the monastery and placed it in a sarcophagus between the altar of Saint John the Baptist and the wall. Where also later, by the merits of the same, the Lord deemed it worthy to manifest miracles worthy of remembrance.

**CHAPTER X.** *A mute and deaf man was healed at his tomb.*

Finally, at one time, a deaf and mute man came to the monastery with some from nearby places for the sake of prayer. And since he had been deprived of both speech and hearing from early childhood, he wore two tablets hanging from his neck, with which, by the collision and sound, he sought the mercy of God, which he could not express with voice. When he entered the church with his companions, and saw them placing pieces of wax at each altar, as is the custom of the poor, he approached the tomb of the man of God, placed the tablets he was carrying on top, and prostrated himself as if to pray before it; and immediately, overcome by a deep sleep, as he later recounted, he saw a certain old man, with a shining face and glorious monastic habit, coming forth from the tomb, saying to him: "O man, why are you being weighed down by sleep here?" And when he could not respond at all to the question, the elder said to him: "Rise, and know that I have obtained for you a remedy for the troubles you have suffered until now." Therefore, leaving the tablets there and departing quickly from the monastery, he was instructed not to reveal the gift granted to him by God in this place to anyone. When he awoke and rose, he hastily left the monastery, and as evening was falling, he turned aside to the hospitality of a certain powerful man named Ratgozi. When he was asked by him whence he came, he recounted in order where, when, and how he had received the gift of health. But the man, not believing his account, ordered him to be detained and guarded, and he himself, to inquire more certainly about the truth of the matter, came to the monastery that same night and found the tablets placed on the tomb. He also found the companions healed, who, still unaware of the same event, he diligently inquired whether they had had such a man in their company coming to the monastery: and immediately from their account, he discovered that what he had heard at home was true. This matter became known more quickly to those present and has reached us even to this day through a true report.

**CHAPTER XI.** *How light appeared in the same place given from heaven.*

A certain priest from the congregation named Tanco, while performing the duties of a custodian in the same church, used to enter the basilica at night to replenish the lamps, and he found nearly everything extinguished three times. When he reached the tomb of the holy man, he found a burning candle beside it, and knowing that the splendor of that light was administered from heaven, he did not dare to extinguish it. However, when he departed, the light that had come on its own was also taken away on its own. Moreover, as a sign of a greater miracle, the fire indeed burned in the candle, but the wax did not seem to diminish at all from this heat. The same venerable priest, confirming this often by his account, dispelled all arguments of doubt with this act of truth.

**CHAPTER XII.** *How a certain man, desperate by chance, was easily healed.*

At another time, while the roof of the same church was necessarily being restored due to old age, a certain member of the monastery, burdened with tiles which he was to carry to the top of the basilica, fell from the height of the roof above the man of God's tomb; and soon another immense weight of wood, struck by the falling, covered him from above. When those standing by rushed to him, believing him already dead, to perform the funeral rites, after removing the weight of the wood for a short while, he lay showing no movement of his limbs;

and then, taking a long breath, he rose unharmed without any injury, and returned joyfully to the labor he had begun. In this miracle, without a doubt, the merits of the holy Father were made clear, since the height of the roof from which the aforementioned man had fallen was suspended no less than forty feet from the ground, and the weight following the falling could have covered him in a way that would suffice for the oppression of many men, but could not crush him.

**CHAPTER XIII.** *A contracted person restored to health.*

At another time, a certain blind man arrived and was received into the hospitality prepared for the poor; and on the same night, when he wanted to go to the church, the boy who was supposed to guide him refused his help due to the excessive cold. As he was greatly pained that he did not merit to participate in such a solemnity (for it was the vigil of Sunday), a certain young man, so contracted in all his limbs that he could not move in any way except by crawling on his hands, lay in the same place. Compassionate of his pain, he pulled himself from his bed and guided the blind man's steps with whatever comfort he could provide. As they entered the church, they accidentally came to the tomb of Othmar. For the blind man thought that his benevolent predecessor had left some door open in that corner through which they could enter the nearby crypt. Therefore, unexpectedly striking against the sarcophagus of the man of God, which was a little higher than the ground, he suddenly recoiled and fell to the ground, filling the whole space of the church with terrifying cries. The blind man, hearing this, thinking that his guide was being seized by madness, tried to flee as best he could. But the merciful Lord, the author and lover of all good, because he saw the weak boy wanting to perform an act of piety beyond his strength, and by the merits of blessed Othmar obtaining it, deemed it worthy to reward his goodwill with the gift of health. For immediately, with his limbs restored to their state, he led the blind man, whom he had just dragged to the church on his hands, through the other places of prayer in that same area with firm steps; and because he stayed in the monastery for some time afterward, he declared the same to all, even to those who had been less present at this act, so that no one thereafter could doubt it.

**CHAPTER XIV.** *Earth turned to stone.*
A certain scholar stealthily took a piece of wax from the tomb of blessed Othmar. However, upon returning to the inn, as he belittled what he had done, he immediately recognized his error, confused by God's clear correction of his folly. For when he brought forth the same piece from his bosom, he found it changed into the hardness of stone. And when he joined obstinacy to his rashness, he hid this deed from everyone for a long time, except for him who was aware of the same things at that time, and this person is the most faithful relator of the miracle we have recounted.

**CHAPTER XV.** *A cleric's hands restored.*
At another time, a certain cleric came, to whom the use of both hands had been denied in a most miserable way. For with his fingers twisted and his nails sunk into the bones of his palms, he was tormented by excessive pains without interruption, to the point that certain parts of his hands had rotted and emitted a strong stench. As he stood not far from the tomb of the holy man, suddenly his fingers began to rise individually in order and return to the natural harmony of their actions. He, who should have rejoiced at the granted gift of health, testified to the magnitude of his pain with a horrible cry, and at that very hour, with his hands fully restored, he subsequently departed in health.

**CHAPTER XVI.** *How the same tomb remained unharmed in the destruction of the basilica, and how the relics of the holy man were transferred to a high place.*
What has recently taken place concerning the tomb of the same holy man, when the church of St. Gall was being destroyed for the sake of rebuilding, we believe should not be kept silent. In that same basilica, next to the altar of Saint John the Baptist, there was a certain

chest built against the wall with not large stones, constructed with masonry on four sides, and above it, boards of three or four fingers in thickness were placed transversely and covered with mortar, in which the little body of the holy man lay elevated slightly above the floor on a wooden plank. Therefore, many, estimating that the body of the holy Father was buried underground, believed that the construction of the chest was merely to designate the place of burial, and thus thinking that the tomb could remain intact, they attacked the walls of the church with machines, compelling them to fall with frequent blows of battering rams. Although they were of great height from every side, nearly collapsing under the great impacts of the machines, they were miraculously not harmed in any part of the chest. After the ashes were removed, it was found intact from every side, as if it had not been struck by the falling walls. However, later, when a certain person carelessly threw a not large stone upon it, it was immediately broken on one side. Finally, having learned that the relics of the holy Father were in it, they transferred them with great honor and placed them in the church of Saint Peter behind the altar.

**CHAPTER XVII.** *What vision was revealed in that oratory to a certain brother.*

After a few days had passed, a certain brother, while anticipating the nocturnal vigils, had entered that oratory one night for the sake of prayer, and with all his heart he directed his prayers at the altar, when he saw a person standing on the right side of the altar, shining with angelic brightness, indeed adorned in priestly attire, with his face turned toward the east, exhibiting the posture of intense prayer: he asserted that the very garments were of such brightness that they would dazzle human weakness. As he gazed at this for a long time, and was anxiously weighing whether he should approach closer, the person who had appeared withdrew, leaving him astonished and amazed by the miracle. Therefore, it is not incredible that the same venerable man wished to declare his presence through this vision, as a sign of the repeated devotion of the brother concerning his translation.

# Life of St. Othmar (Latin)

**PROLOGUS.** *Ad fratres monasterii Sancti Galli.*

Finitis duobus libellis quos de vita et virtutibus beati Galli confessoris juxta fidem quae vel scripto vel dicto ad nos usque pervenerat, vere potius quam lepide composuimus; jubentibus vobis, fratres charissimi, qui in coenobio ejusdem sancti Patris constituti, fervoris ejus quem in Dei rebus habuit, sancti strenuitate propositi specimen exhibetis, libet subnectere eam relationem, quae de sancti Patris Othmari studiis et virtutibus per ejus merita ostensis vestra assertione et cura litteris est mandata veracibus: quae cum sit veritate plena, ratione perspicua, non ob aliud a nobis est iterata, nisi quia charissimus frater Gozbertus qui idem opusculum edidit, cujus charitati quidquam negare nec volumus nec debemus, id ut fieret postulavit, imo praecepit, quem etiam in hac occupatione instantissimum ergodiocten sine taedio laeti sustinuimus. Itaque lectori credulo sufficiat haec abbreviatio nostra; incredulus autem qui fuerit, ad eam conscriptionem quam sequimur recurrens, multiplici astipulatione testium conventus ad fidem, si gratus est, segnis non erit.

**CAPUT PRIMUM.** *Quomodo vir Dei Othmarus pro sanctitate vitae cellulae sancti Galli sit praelatus, et regia auctoritate regularem inibi vitam instituerit.*

Igitur Othmarus, genere Alamannorum oriundus, in aetate puerili a fratre suo Raetiam Curiensem perductus est, et in servitio Victoris, earumdem partium comitis, multo tempore constitutus, et litterarum scientia sublimatus, virtutum sectator morumque laudabilium possessor, sacerdotii gradum conscendit, et a supradicto comite benigne retentus, cuidam titulo sancti Florini confessoris praelatus est. Cumque morum ejus probitas et sanctae vitae munditia longe lateque plurimorum aures rumore dulci respergeret, Waltramnus quidam qui sibi vastitatem eremi, in qua sanctus Gallus cellulam construxerat, velut a parentibus haereditario ad se jure transmissam vindicavit, eumdem Othmarum a Victore supradicto ad praeficiendum eidem cellulae postulavit; et voti compos effectus, cellulam cum omnibus quae ad eam pertinebant, illi solemniter commendavit. Atque ut sui melius desiderii convalesceret utilitas, ad Pippinum regem profectus, eumdem abbatem ipsi praesentavit, et locum cui eum pridem praefecerat, proprietatis jure principi contradidit, omni instantia deposcens ut regia auctoritate ex integro Othmarus abbas eidem praeficeretur loco. Cujus petitioni jam dictus princeps assensum praebens, locum sibi traditum viro venerabili commendavit, et regularem inibi vitam instituere jussit. At ille regressus, confestim boni mandritae studium in ipso exsecutus initio, undique versum congrua monachis habitacula construxit, et ipsius sacri loci statum ad utilitatem divini servitii studiosissime reformavit. Religiosos etiam quosque ita liberalitate sua ad devotionis studium invitavit, ut ex quorumdam donationibus possessiones ipsius coenobii admodum dilataret, et infra paucos annos complures ad sacrae militiam vitae attractos magisterio suo et cura decentissime gubernaret.

**CAPUT II.** *Qua conversationis sanctae perfectione nituerit.*

His praelibatis, vitae ejus sanctitatem liceat summatim perstringere, ut liquido cunctis clareat quibus profectuum gradibus ad hanc gloriam sit evectus. Erat denique parcimoniae sector eximius, creberrimo macerans jejunio corpus, ita ut in praecipuis jejuniorum diebus ex consuetudine bidui abstinentiam continuaret frequentius. Et his contra tentamentorum jacula clypeis praemunitus vigilias amabat, et assiduitate orandi spiritalia nequitiae repellebat. Summae autem humilitatis gratia praecipue praeditus, in tantum voluntariam paupertatem diligebat, ut terrenam gloriam omnibus fugeret modis. Cui etiam haec erat consuetudo, ut si quoquam pro utilitate monasterii eum tendere necessitas poposcisset, vilis miti dorso veheretur aselli. Erat inter caetera tanta in eo pauperum sollicitudo, ut eorum curam per se potius quam per alios exhibere studeret. In eo vero misericordiae opere quod eleemosyna dicitur, vix cuiquam habebatur secundus. Nam ad suscipiendos leprosos, qui a caeteris hominibus sejuncti manere semotim consueverunt, hospitiolum haud longe a monasterio extra eas mansiones quibus caeteri pauperes recipiebantur constituit, et eis curam per se omnimodis impendebat ita sollicite, ut nocturnis etiam horis monasterio saepe digressus, curam infirmitati eorum miro devotionis adhiberet obsequio. Capita siquidem eorum pedesque abluens, purulenta suis manibus vulnera detergebat, et victui necessaria ministrabat, illam semper animo revolvens sententiam quam justus Judex misericordibus prolaturus est dicens: Quod uni ex minimis fratribus meis fecistis, mihi fecistis (Matth. XXV). Sicque factum est ut cunctorum qui eum noverant veneratione sublimis, Pater pauperum appellaretur a pluribus. Quem tam pleniter misericordiae studium possederat, ut si quem pauperum nuditatis injuria torpentem conspiceret, plerumque suis exutus vestibus, miseri contegeret artus, ita ut interdum sine tunica, sola cappa contectus ad monasterium remearet. Maluit enim per praesentis pompae contemptum ad indumentum incorruptionis aeternae pertingere, quam per boni operis amissionem futurae nuditatis opprobria sustinere.

**CAPUT III.** *Quantam in pauperes misericordiam habuerit.*

Quodam etiam tempore ad Pippinum regem veniens, honorifice susceptus est, et inter alia largitatis ejus beneficia, ad necessitates fratrum suorum sublevandas argenti libras septuaginta percepit. Sed mox ut ad sua rediret egressus, maximam ejusdem pecuniae partem prae foribus palatii pauperibus erogavit. Paucos autem solidos vix a fratribus qui secum erant compulsus retinuit, quibus postmodum quoddam territorium monasterio vicinum coemit. Dominicorum enim non immemor mandatorum, sui causa de crastino non cogitabat, sciens monachum victu et tegumento contentum esse debere: et ideo paupertatem sibi potius suisque delegit, quam rerum transeuntium possessionem superfluam, expeditis mentibus onerosam.

**CAPUT IV.** *Qualiter a quibusdam iniquis pro zelo justitiae, quo fervebat, multis affectus sit contumeliis.*

Igitur cum jam Dominus meritis ejus digna rependere decrevisset, callidus universae bonitatis inimicus bonis ejus actibus invidens, ejusque exemplis aliorum vitam dolens proficere, quietem quam in Christi servitio licet non parum laborando possedit, perturbare contendit. Sed, quamvis flatibus temporariae adversitatis pulsata, radicem petrae veritatis habens infixam, paradisi cedrus inconvulsa permansit. Nam Warinus et Ruadhardus, qui tunc temporis totius Alamanniae curam administrabant, diabolo suadente, immanissimo avaritiae morbo praeventi, res ecclesiarum sub sua potestate sitarum magna ex parte in proprietatis suae dominium per vim contraxerunt. Qui cum sibi de possessionibus B. Galli perplura eodem violentiae ausu vindicassent, vir Dei Othmarus non possessionibus terrenis inhians, sed coenobialis vitae in eodem loco rerum ingruente penuria defectum praemetuens, Pippinum regem adiit, ipsique tyrannicam eorum praesumptionem exposuit, pariter protestatus grave eum crimen incursurum si eorum actibus consentiendo faveret. Qua pro causa benevolus princeps utrumque conveniens, interminatus est eis gratia sua illos omnimodis carituros si non ecclesiae Dei quae injuste abstulerant, absque recrastinatione restituerent. At illi patriam repetentes, vitio rapacitatis infecti et bestiali saevitia efferati, jussionem regiam neglexerunt: virum etiam Dei Othmarum, cum pro hac re iterum principem adire vellet, missis post eum clanculum militibus, vinculis injectum per vim reduci fecerunt; necnon et Lambertum quemdam, qui fratribus ejus professione connumeratus erat, non vitae sanctitate, persuaserunt ut ei ficta quadam machinatione crimen luxuriae impingeret, id elaborantes ut, sanctitate ejus hujusmodi suspicionibus infamata, deponendi eum occasionem invenirent. Qua causa plurimi tam dolosae factionis ignari ad concilium sunt evocati.

**CAPUT V.** *Quam in objectione ficti criminis modestiam tenuerit, et qua accusator ejus poena multatus sit.*

Itaque vir venerabilis, castae integer vitae ac morum maturitate grandaevus, in medio concilii collocatur, et in ejus accusationem Lambertus falsitatis minister coram omnibus praesentatur: acceptaque loquendi licentia veritatis oblitus, falsitatis assertor dixit se quamdam feminam nosse quae a viro beato vim pollutionis fuisset perpessa. Ad quod fertur nullum dedisse responsum. Cumque plurimis respondere cogeretur objectis, hujusmodi dicto temperavit eloquium: Fateor, inquiens, me supra modum peccasse in multis, de hujusmodi autem objectione criminis secreti mei inspectorem Deum invoco testem. Illis autem ut hujus facti se excusatione purgaret, attentius ei instantibus, mente securus, conscientia liber, tacitus perduravit. Et quia accusandi licentiam apud judices patere cognovit, maluit pro sinceritate sui pectoris divino quam humano pro excusatione criminis placere judicio. Mox ergo ut cunctis claresceret ipsius castimoniam falso fuisse infamatam, Lambertum ultio divina corripuit. Nam febrium vexatione pervasus, paulatim resoluto membrorum vigore contrahi coepit. Sicque omnibus membris status sui amittentibus rectitudinem vel formam, capite ad terram more quadrupedum inclinato, non solum deformitate figurae terribilis, verum etiam viva voce in sanctum peccasse omni tempore fatebatur.

**CAPUT VI.** *Quomodo inter arcta custodiae claustra vitam finierit.*
Consilio autem inique inchoato et iniquius terminato, vir Dei Othmarus apud villam Potamum palatio inclusus est. Quo cum nullus intrare vel colloqui cum eo permitteretur, aliquot dies absque corporalis sustentaculo victus transegit. Cumque diuturna vexatione famis laboraret, Peragosus [Surio Patgozus] quidam e fratribus ejus noctu advenire solebat, et ei victus solatia ministrare. Postmodum vero Gozbertus quidam, vir potens, dum sibi virum Dei commendari ab iniquis principibus impetrasset, in quadam Rheni fluminis insula nomine Stein juxta praedium suum custodiae illum deputavit: ubi idem sanctus Pater spirituali tantummodo exercitio, id est orationibus ac jejuniis vacans, eo liberius Domino deservivit quo ab humana frequentatione curisque saecularibus fuerat absolutus. His et similibus

notae devotionis insistens operibus, exacto non multi temporis spatio, ab his mundanae perturbationis angustiis ad coelestis latitudinem gaudii, decimo sexto [Chesnio male decimo septimo] Kalendarum Decembrium die commigravit, et corpus ejus in eadem insula tumulatum multis deinceps diebus ibidem sine corruptione permansit.

**CAPUT VII.** *Qualiter post multum temporis corpus ejus sine corruptione repertum sit.*

Evolutis autem post transitum ejus decem annis, fratres illius per visionem a Domino commoniti sunt, ut corpus chari Patris ad monasterium reducerent. Hoc patefacto divinae voluntatis consilio, undecim ex eisdem fratribus noctu ad locum in quo sancti viri exuviae servabantur deveniunt, et sepulcrum aperientes, corpus ejus ab omni corruptione illaesum reperiunt, excepto quod pars extrema pedis unius quam aqua abluebat, tantum colore mutato quasi tabida videbatur. Et congruo satis miraculo prima sanitatis ejus indicia claruerunt, ut videlicet tam illaesum a corruptione corpus illius inveniretur, quam liber ipse luerat a crimine, cujus oppositione superatus videbatur ad tempus. Hac itaque devoti fratres rerum novitate perfectius instructi, corpus honorifice sumptum rati imposuerunt, et accendentes candelas, unam ad caput, alteram collocaverunt ad pedes.

**CAPUT VIII.** *Quam mirabiliter in translatione corporis ejus tempestas sedata sit.*

Cumque deserto littore incertis se profundi viis commisissent, et summa instantia remigio insistentes sub omni celeritate cuperent remeare, continuo tanta vis pluviae et ventorum prorupit, ut vix effugium se crederent habituros. Sed mira omnipotentis Dei dispensatione et (ut credimus) sancti viri meritis actum est, ut ipsa etiam elementa, quae nobis insensibilia videntur, famulantia sui creatoris imperio, quanti viri reliquiae ibidem veherentur sentirent. Nam pelagus circumquaque imbrifera tempestate commotum, undas in altum suspendens, nihil omnino remigantibus molestiae intulit, sed in quamcunque partem navis devenit, rejectis flatibus tumentes in se fluctus depressit. Et ita omni ex parte undarum molibus, imbrium effusionibus, ventorumque flatibus non parvo dimotis spatio, quasi sepe quadam scapha cingebatur, ut ne una quidem pluviae gutta, quae hinc inde vehementer inundabat, in illam descenderet. Cerei quoque qui in beati Patris obsequium ardentes ad caput pedesque fuerant collocati, lumen primae accensionis nequaquam amiserunt, quoadusque corpus ejus ad monasterium deferretur.

**CAPUT IX.** *De abundantia potus coelitus subministrati, et ubi corpus ejus post translationem sit tumulatum.*

Aliud adhuc restat miraculum quod in eadem sacri corporis translatione devotis fratribus Dominus patefecit. Nam cum ex nimia remigandi instantia fessi, adveniente refectionis hora ad recuperandas alimento corporeo vires, laudibus Domini praemissis consedissent, tandemque felici convivio intermisceri potus solatia commonerent, unus ministrorum intulit nihil ibi jam potuum superesse, praeter quod in flascone parvo servabatur, unde vix unicuique quippiam ad gustandum potiusquam ad bibendum praeberi potuisset. Illi vero miraculorum Domini, quomodo paucis panibus multitudinem bominum paverit numerosam, facientes mentionem, ex eodem parvo quod habebant, cunctis qui aderant cum charitate distribui fecerunt. Et mirum in modum coepit in eodem vasculo ita liquoris haustus crescere, ut continua effusione nihil minui videretur, quoadusque bibentes poculorum copia vincerentur. Ergo, pro rei novitate obstupefacti, largitori omnium bonorum Domino, qui eis tam mirabiliter sufficientiam praebuit, debitas gratiarum actiones cum laudibus persolverunt. Statimque ut iter coeptum itidem aggressi sunt, in vasculo potus cessavit. Cumque optati littoris portum subissent, fratribus qui obviam cum Dei laudibus venerunt, quae gesta fuerant ex ordine retexerunt; celebratoque in commune gaudio, sancti viri corpus magno sumptum cum honore ad monasterium transtulerunt, et inter aram sancti Joannis Baptistae et parietem in sarcophago posuerunt. Ubi etiam postmodum ipsius facientibus meritis memoria digna Dominus dignatus est manifestare miracula.

CAPUT X. *Mutus et surdus ad sepulcrum ejus est curatus.*

Denique quodam tempore surdus et mutus cum quibusdam de vicinis locis orationis causa monasterium adeuntibus venit. Et quia a primaeva aetate et locutionis et auditus carebat officiis, tabellas duas collo dependentes gestabat, quarum collisione et sonitu misericordiae opus, quod voce nequibat, precabatur. Is cum suis conviatoribus ecclesiam ingressus, dum eos singulis altaribus particulas cerae, sicuti pauperum est consuetudo, imponere conspiceret, ad viri Dei sepulcrum accedens, tabulas quas gestabat desuper posuit, seseque quasi oraturus ante illud prostravit; et protinus alto sopore depressus, ut ipse postmodum retulit, senem quemdam facie nitidum, monachico habitu gloriosum, quasi e tumulo vidit procedere dicentem sibi: O homo, cur hic sopore deprimeris? Cumque ad interrogata nihil penitus respondere potuisset, senior ad eum dixit: Surge, et incommodorum quibus hactenus laborasti, remedium a me tibi impetratum scias. Ergo tabulis istic dimissis confestimque monasterio decedens, donum a Deo tibi concessum in hoc loco nemini pandas. Qui cum evigilans surrexisset, sub magna festinatione monasterio digressus, inclinato jam die vesperi ad cujusdam Ratgozi potentis viri hospitium divertit. Cumque ab illo interrogaretur unde veniret, per ordinem exposuit, ubi, quando et quomodo sanitatis donum fuisset adeptus. At ille narrationi ejus non credens, teneri eum et custodiri praecepit, ipseque veritatem rei certius inquisiturus, eadem nocte ad monasterium venit, et tabulas super tumulum positas reperit. Conviatores quoque sanati cum invenisset adhuc ejusdem facti ignaros, diligenter ab illis inquisivit, si talem hominem monasterium pergentes in comitatu habuissent: et continuo ex eorum narratione vera esse quae domi audierat deprehendit. Quae res et praesentibus citius innotuit, et ad nos usque relatione veridica pervenit.

CAPUT XI. *Quomodo lux in eodem loco coelitus data apparuerit.*

Presbyter quidam ex ipsa congregatione nomine Tanco, dum in eadem Ecclesia custodis officium gereret, nocturnae quietis tempore pro reficiendis luminaribus basilicam solitus introire, tribus vicibus pene omnia reperit exstincta. Ad sancti autem viri sepulcrum perveniens, ardentem cereum juxta illud invenit, sciensque luminis illius administrari coelitus splendorem, exstinguere non praesumpsit. Ut vero discessit, lux quae per se venerat, per se etiam subtracta est. Ubi et ad majoris indicium miraculi, ignis quidem in candela solito rutilabat, cerae vero nihil per hunc ardorem minui videbatur. Haec idem venerabilis presbyter saepius sua relatione confirmans, omne dubitationis argumentum ab hoc facto veritatis ratione depellit.

**CAPUT XII.** *Quidam ibidem casu desperatus quam facile convaluerit.*

Quodam etiam tempore, dum ejusdem ecclesiae tecta vetustate dilapsa necessario restaurarentur, quidam ex ipsius monasterii familia tegularum quas ad fastigia basilicae deferre debuerat, onere praegravatus, de ipsa tecti altitudine supra viri Dei corruit sepulcrum: moxque immensum aliud lignorum pondus corruentis impulsum attactu in ipso eum casus exitio desuper operuit. Cumque astantes occurrerent, ut ei quem jam exanimem crediderunt, funeris debita persolverent, sublato lignorum pondere aliquantisper, nullos membrorum motus ostendens jacuit; ac deinde per longa suspiria halitum resumens, absque ulla laesione surrexit incolumis, et ad incoepti operis laborem rediit gaudens. In hoc ergo miraculo haud dubie sancti Patris merita claruerunt, cum et altitudo tecti unde supradictus homo ceciderat, non minus quadraginta pedum mensura a terra esset suspensa, et pondus insequens corruentem quod ad multorum hominum oppressionem sufficeret, operire praecipitem, non conterere potuisset.

**CAPUT XIII.** *Contractus sanitati restitutus.*

Alio tempore caecus quidam adveniens, hospitio pauperum necessitatibus praeparato susceptus est; et nocte eadem cum ecclesiam vellet adire puerulus qui ei ducatum praebere debuerat, ob nimiam frigoris asperitatem officii sui negavit juvamen. Cumque nimis doleret quod tantae solemnitati interesse non mereretur (erant quippe Dominicae diei vigiliae), adolescens quidam ita membris omnibus contractus, ut non aliter quoquam incedere quam manibus reptando potuisset; cum in eodem loco quiesceret, ejus dolori compassus de lecto se protraxit, et quali potuit solatio caeci vestigia rexit. Ut ergo ecclesiam intraverunt, utili errore ad sepulcrum Othmari venere. Putabat etenim iisdem benevolus caeci praecessor in ipso angulo aliquod ostium patere, per quod cryptam eidem loco vicinam intrare potuissent. Itaque ex improviso in sarcophagum viri Dei quia paulo altius eminebat a terra impingens, subito resiliit, et ad terram protinus concidit, totiusque ecclesiae spatia horrentibus implevit clamoribus. Caecus vero haec audiens, ductorem suum insania aestimans agitari, prout poterat aufugere studuit. Misericors autem Dominus totius boni auctor et amator, quia viderat debilem puerum ultra vires opus pietatis exhibere voluisse, beati Othmari etiam meritis id obtinentibus, benevolentiam ejus dono sanitatis remunerare dignatus est. Nam protinus in statum suum membris restitutis, caecum quem paulo ante manibus reptans ad ecclesiam traxit, firmatis jam gressibus per caetera in eodem ambitu orationis loca deduxit; et quia aliquandiu postea in ipso monasterio mansit, ita omnibus etiam qui huic facto minus interfuerant, idipsum declaravit, ut de eo nulli deinceps licuerit dubitare.

**CAPUT XIV.** *Terra in lapidem conversa.*

Quidam de numero scholasticorum ab eodem beati Othmari tumulo particulam cerae furtim subtraxit. Regressus autem ad hospitium cum parvipenderet quod commisit, statim manifesta Dei correctione stultitiae suae errorem confusus agnovit. Nam cum eamdem particulam de sinu proferret, in lapidis duritiam eam reperit commutatam. Cumque temeritati obstinationem junxisset, multo tempore hoc factum a cunctorum agnitione abscondit, praeter eum videlicet qui et earumdem rerum tunc erat conscius, et hoc in tempore miraculi quod retulimus relator exstat fidelissimus.

**CAPUT XV.** *Clerico cuidam manus restitutae.*

Alio quoque tempore clericus quidam advenit, cui utriusque manus officium miserabili prorsus modo fuerat denegatum. Nam contortis in volam digitis unguibusque ad ossa usque palmarum immersis, nimiis sine intermissione cruciabatur miser doloribus, ita ut etiam quaedam partes manuum putrefactae gravem longius fetorem emitterent. Is cum non longe beati viri tumulo consisteret, subito coeperunt digiti ejus singulatim ex ordine erigi, et ad naturalium concordiam actionum redire. Ipse vero qui pro concesso sanitatis dono gaudere debuerat, doloris magnitudinem clamore horribili testabatur, et eadem hora, manibus ad integrum restitutis, postmodum sanus abscessit.

**CAPUT XVI.** *Quomodo idem sepulcrum in destructione basilicae illaesum permanserit, et qualiter in altum locum reliquiae viri sancti translatae sint.*

Quid nuper quoque circa ejusdem viri sancti sepulcrum gestum sit, quando ecclesia B. Galli reaedificandi causa destruebatur, arbitramur non esse silentio supprimendum. In eadem basilica, juxta aram beati Joannis Baptistae, arca quaedam parieti contigua non magnis lapidibus opere caementicio in quatuor lateribus constructa, superius autem tabulis, quarum grossitudo trium vel quatuor erat digitorum, in transversum positis caementoque desuper litis cooperta videbatur, in qua sancti viri corpusculum paulo altius a pavimento sublevatum tabula lignea tantum supposita jacebat. Aestimantes igitur multi corpus sancti Patris sub terra positum, arcae vero constructionem ad designandum tantummodo sepulturae locum caementatam, ideo tumulum remanere intactum posse credentes, muros ecclesiae machinis aggressi crebris arietum ictibus ruere compulerunt. Qui cum ex omni parte magnae altitudinis essent, magnis machinarum impulsibus pariter pene corruentes, sepulcro viri Dei superferrentur, mirum in modum nullam arcae particulam laeserunt. Quae evectis cineribus sic intacta ex omni parte reperta est, ac si nullo cadentium impetu parietum impetita fuisset. Postea vero dum quidam saxum haud grande super eam incaute jecisset, protinus quadam ex parte confracta est. Tandem itaque cognito quod in ea reliquiae sancti Patris haberentur, cum magno eas honore inde transtulerunt, et in ecclesia beati Petri post altare posuerunt.

**CAPUT XVII.** *Quae ostensio in eodem oratorio cuidam fratri manifestata sit.*

Paucis deinde diebus exactis, quidam frater dum nocturnas vigilias praeveniens idem oratorium orandi gratia quadam nocte fuisset ingressus, totoque affectu precibus insistens ad altare direxisset intentum, nescio quam a dextris altaris in angelicae claritatis nitore vidit stare personam, sacerdotali quidem habitu praefulgentem, facie autem ad orientem versa, gestu corporis intentissimae orationis specimen exhibentem: vestimenta vero ipsa tanti fuisse nitoris asseruit, ut humanae infirmitatis reverberarent obtutus. Cumque haec diu conspiceret, et utrum propius deberet accedere anxia mentis agitatione trutinaret, persona quae apparuerat se subtrahens, eum miraculo et stupore consternatum reliquit. Non est igitur incredibile eumdem venerabilem virum praesentiae suae visione declarare voluisse, digne circa translationem suam fraternae devotionis iteratam fuisse solertiam.

This work was produced in association with:

www.ingramcontent.com/pod-product-compliance
Lightning Source LLC
LaVergne TN
LVHW061049070526
838201LV00074B/5239